Reflections for the Effective Staff Fund Raiser

A volume of the Effective Philanthropy and
Fund Raising series.

Reflections for the Effective Staff Fund Raiser

Quotes, axioms and observations to help you run our important institutions

Jim Norvell

Writers Club Press

San Jose New York Lincoln Shanghai

Reflections for the Effective Staff Fund Raiser
Quotes, axioms and observations to help you run our important institutions

Writers Club Press
an imprint of iUniverse, Inc.

For information address:
iUniverse, Inc.
5220 S. 16th St., Suite 200
Lincoln, NE 68512
www.iuniverse.com

Artistic license was exercised with the quotes borrowed from an illustrious array of thoughtful people. Insertion of their observations in juxtaposition to my own was based on their unique similarity, often taken out of context. Those who are still around to do so are free to do the same with mine.

ISBN: 0-595-20881-9

Printed in the United States of America

A Professional Bow

If you spend a lifetime in philanthropy, you will undoubtedly encounter a special breed of fund-raising manager that you know would have succeeded in any line of work—competent, amiable, inspirational, articulate and visionary. It is sheer folly to isolate examples from a thirty-year career, but no one ever accused me of good judgment. So here goes. I will recognize three.

Carole Lewis is hard-wired into the social and political leadership of Oregon. Her family's commercial and financial holdings place them among the elite wealth of the West Coast. She could have had her pick of positions in any of the family businesses, but she became development director of Oregon Public Broadcasting (OPB). Working under two presidents she organized and managed the transition of OPB from derelict quarters to a new broadcast center by harnessing powerful leadership and greatly increasing private support. The level of commitment and professionalism that she brought to the effort earned the respect of both employees and donors.

Barbara Grady was enjoying a full social whirl and the competition of club tennis after sending two grown children into the world when a friend asked her to be the secretary for a building campaign. She was in place when I took over management. Her social skills were invaluable in organizing and conducting an endless calendar of meetings and events. Along the way, she became a confidant, advisor and friend. When the campaign ended successfully two years later, I recommended her for the new director of development position. In one of the executive officer's rare mistakes he hired a young man instead. In two short months the error was evident and Barbara was elevated to the job, which she held for the next 12 years and through two additional (and successful) capital campaigns.

Cliff Hoffman's adventures in philanthropy began when he left college coaching to become a capital campaign director. Through several campaigns and family moves he earned his spurs before settling down to a desk job at a hospital in Tacoma, Washington. In the 1980s he become president of the California Hospital Medical Center Foundation, just south of downtown Los Angeles. For over a decade, Cliff has been more than a hospital fund raiser—he has been a community leader, helping to expand services and improve the lives of largely Hispanic immigrant families working their way out of poverty. Cliff deserves credit for his fundraising success but plaudits for his humanity. I have never met a person more generous or selfless, and never a better professional friend.

Jim Norvell

For my father who had the bearing, demeanor and commitment of a first-rate professional throughout his fund-raising career.

Talent develops in quiet places, character in the full current of human life.

Johann Wolfgang von Goethe

Quotes, axioms and observations to help you expand our important institutions

This book was compiled as a resource for nonprofit staff members. It contains some of the key guidelines I have found to be useful in managing nonprofit organizations and keeping participants motivated. It also provides some neat quotations that may be used in various pieces of organizational literature to motivate volunteers and staff. Finally, I wrote it because I like quotes and have found that many of you share that enjoyment.

Good management seeks to eliminate insecurity.

One can never creep when one feels an impulse to soar.

Helen Keller

A good executive encourages numerous contacts between board and staff.

Always be smarter than the people who hired you.

Lena Horne

Organizations that work in integrative and non-judgmental ways create synergy.

Enthusiasm always exaggerates the importance of important things and overlooks the differences.

Hugh Stevenson Tigner

The chief executive and the chief development officer share a close relationship with the board.

Sharing is sometimes more demanding than giving.

Mary Catherine Bateton

Conflict allows manipulative people to control organizations for their own purposes.

Such is the human race, often it seems a pity that Noah didn't miss the boat.

Mark Twain

The best chief financial officer will think like a development officer and vice versa.

It's not the employer who pays the wages—he only handles the money. It is the product that pays the wages.

Henry Ford

Threats seldom loom suddenly, they creep up from shoddy governance and weak management.

Bureaucracy defends the status quo long past the time when the quo has lost its status.

Lawrence J. Peter

Conflicting objectives and competing agendas make optimization an unreasonable standard.

In this world there are only two tragedies. One is not getting what one wants, and the other is getting it.

Oscar Wilde

The same fireworks that sell fiction, illuminate nonprofits and often create serious problems.

It is with our passions as it is with fire and water—they are good servants but bad masters.

Roger L'Strange

Ambiguity frightens those who believe that decision-making is a wholly rational exercise.

Reality is nothing but a collective hunch.

Lily Tomlin

Organizational structure must allow for control.

Discipline is the soul of an army. It makes small numbers formidable, procures success to the weak, and esteem to all.

George Washington

Delegation of authority is fundamental to organizational control.

Never tell people how to do things. Tell them what to do and they will surprise you with their integrity.

General George S. Patton, Jr.

The number of direct subordinates governs a manager's sphere of control.

What you cannot enforce.
Do not command.

Sophocles

Discipline falters quickly when lines of authority are unclear or overlap.

Confusion is a word we have invented for an order which is not understood.

Henry Miller

Weak managers tend to use authority as a security blanket.

Authority is never without hate.

Euripides

Commitment to shared values shapes the organizational culture.

If you don't have a shared value system,
you don't have an inner source of security.

Stephen R. Covey

The ideal nonprofit is professionally managed and volunteer led.

The test of a first-rate intelligence is the ability to hold two opposed ideas in the mind at the same time, and still retain the ability to function.

F. Scott Fitzgerald

Fund raising is best managed by experienced professionals and done by respected volunteers.

When the professional's fund-raising knowledge and management skills are combined with the volunteer's influence, the result is success.

James Gregory Lord

Nonprofit management is more difficult than private-sector management.

[Nonprofits] need effective leadership and management a good deal more than even businesses do.

Peter F. Drucker

Aggressive recruitment and retention of top performers is essential for success.

*Authority tends to assign jobs
to those least able to do them.*

Cornuelle's Law

Relatively weak authority and reliance on volunteers heavily tax the "people skills" of nonprofit leaders.

Certainty generally is illusion,
and repose is not the destiny of man.

Oliver Wendell Holmes, Jr.

Skilled fund-raising management dictates success; good intentions alone breed failure.

The winds and the waves are always on the side of the ablest navigator.

Edward Gibbon

Fund-raising records are the basis of performance evaluation.

The more extensive a man's knowledge of what has been done, the greater will be his power of knowing what to do.

Benjamin Disraeli

Accurate records are the only kind that work.

Blessed are those who can give without remembering, and take without forgetting.

Elizabeth Bibesco

Poorly maintained records weaken all other performance.

Order marches with weighty and measured strides; disorder is always in a hurry.

Napoleon I

Time is an enemy of accuracy.

Time is a dressmaker specializing in alterations.

Faith Baldwin

Recall and respect are essential attributes of those entrusted with donor records.

Computers are useless. They can only give you answers.

Pablo Picasso

Second only to listing at the proper gift level is need to accurately spell the donor's name.

First you forget names, then you forget faces,
then you forget to pull your zipper up,
then you forget to pull your zipper down.

Leo Rosenberg

Donors expect recipient organizations to be appreciative enough to spell their names correctly.

I think the one lesson I have learned is that there is no substitute for paying attention.

Diane Sawyer

Donors trust that their contributions will be spent wisely, but they like assurance.

*When a man accepts a public trust,
he should consider himself as public
property.*

Thomas Jefferson

Complete records of a fund-raising campaign are the cornerstone of the next campaign.

*Our heritage is composed of all the voices
that can answer our questions.*

Andre Malraux

Nonprofits need and deserve professional management, but volunteers must have a central role.

Management, however wise its genius may be, can do nothing without the privileges which the community affords.

W. L. Mackenzie King

Nonprofits that lack strong fund-raising skills are destined to live hand-to-mouth.

The trouble with being poor is that it takes up all of your time.

Willem de Kooning

A weak fund-raising board is a deficiency that no paid fundraiser can overcome.

Life is something like a trumpet.
If you don't put anything in, you won't get
anything out.

W. C. Handy

Insensitivity and arrogance are undesirable traits, in a development officer they are poison.

There are two kinds of people in the world—Those who walk into a room and say, "There you are" and those who say, "Here I am."

Abigail Van Buren

Donors have rights that organizations should look upon as obligations.

There's no such thing as a free lunch.

Milton Friedman

Marketing creates constituents and bonds with them.

You can get everything in life you want if you will just help enough other people get what they want.

Zig Ziglar

An organization must reflect the values associated with the service it provides and the constituency it seeks.

Tell me thy company, and I'll tell you what thou art.

Miguel de Cervantes

Awareness of constituents' needs allows a
tighter bond with them.

If you live with a cripple, you will learn to limp.

Plutarch

Nonprofits compete with vacations, second homes, baubles and hobbies.

To vie is not to rival.

Benjamin Disraeli

All objects of consumption have competition.

The real competition of the Red Cross is not that afforded by any other drive. It is the competition of golf club expenses and entertaining and new fur coats and movies and television sets.

Robert Keith Leavitt

Key words trigger deeper levels of discrimination between competing influences.

A mighty flame followeth a tiny spark.

Dante

The concept of equity allows relative value
to be attached to people, objects and ideas.

When you sit with a nice girl for two hours, you think it's only a minute. But when you sit on a hot stove for a minute, you think it's two hours. That's relativity.

Albert Einstein

Unique organizational strengths are leverageable equities.

Jim Palmer's won 240 games, but it took a picture of him standing in his underwear to get nationally known.

Mike Flanagan

The secret of marketing is not out-thinking prospects, it's thinking with them.

I have striven not to laugh at human actions, not to weep at them, nor hate them, but to understand them.

Benedict Spinoza

Positioning tactics are important in creating "luck."

Luck is a matter of preparation meeting opportunity.

Oprah Winfrey

No technological wizardry will sell an
unwanted service to an uninterested market.

If Thomas Wolfe sold,
I'd write Thomas Wolfe.

Mickey Spillane

Defining solutions in terms of values creates demand.

Nobody ever buys a Buick because General Motors needs the money.

Harold J. "Si" Seymour

To stand out, an organization must demonstrate a favorable distinction from the competition.

What we must decide is perhaps how are we valuable, rather than how valuable we are.

F. Scott Fitzgerald

Positioning is the transmission of specific values to gain marketing advantage.

The subconscious is especially receptive to goals in line with our deeper aspirations and values.

Peter M. Senge

Nonprofit organizations use direct mail for more than fund raising.

If a fellow wants to be a nobody in the business world, let him neglect sending the mailman to somebody on his behalf.

Charles Franklin Kettering

An organization's case must "grab" the constituency.

That's our function in life. To make a declarative statement.

Corinne Jacker

The case for support must show organizational strength across the board.

Send them our latitude and longitude.

Adm. William Halsey (answer to enemy's question, "Where is the
American fleet?")

Vision is inspirational when it reflects stakeholders' values.

Man unites himself with the world in the process of creation.

Erich Fromm

The case for support becomes persuasive
through uniqueness, impact and vision.

You see things and you say "Why?"; but I dream things that never were and I say "Why not?"

George Bernard Shaw

The mission is an approach to realizing vision.

Our plans miscarry because they have no aim. When a man does not know what harbor he is making for, no wind is the right wind.

Seneca

The effective case for support links the organization's mission to constituents' values.

It is only with the heart that one can see rightly; what is essential is invisible to the eye.

Antoine de Saint-Expuréy

Major donors respond to performance; reputation alone falls short.

Performance is the ultimate test for any organization.

Peter Drucker

Performance results from a well-conceived mission translated into effective action that society values.

*Action is the only reality, not only reality
but morality as well.*

Abbie Hoffman

Constituents judge the case both historically and comparatively.

He receives hope in future benefit who recognizes a benefit that has already taken place.

Magnus Aurelius Cassiodorus

Linkages between the case for support and constituent values are the basis of an effective case statement.

Every vital development in writing is a development of feeling as well.

T. S. Eliot

Only fully justified needs attract dependable funding.

We must rediscover the distinction between hope and expectation.

Ivan Illich

Verifying no alternative source of funds is a key to justification.

Trust, then verify.

Ronald Reagan

The elimination of alternatives focuses donor prospect attention.

Death and life are not serious alternatives.'

Robinson Jeffers

Fund raising should be based on a realistic projection of the impact the gifts will have.

Give me where to stand, and I will move the earth.

Archimedes

Not all of a nonprofit's identified needs
are equal and some are just not worthy.

Facts are stubborn things; and whatever may be our wishes, our inclinations, or the dictates of our passions, they cannot alter the state of facts and evidence.

John Adams

Organizations gain importance through constituents' interpretation.

The meaning of things is not in the things themselves but in our attitude toward them.

Antoine de Saint-Expuréy

In a mail appeal, the request for money is only part of the message.

Most Americans have never seen the ignorance, degradation, hunger, sickness, and futility in which other Americans live. They won't become involved in economic or political change until something brings the seriousness of the situation home to them.

Shirley Chisholm

Worthiness is a value judgment based on comparative data and experience.

Appreciation is a wonderful thing; it makes what is excellent in others belong to us as well.

Voltaire

Worth is maximized by linking constituent values to organizational performance.

Nothing can have value without being an object of utility.

Karl Marx

Worthiness is not inherent in a nonprofit organization; it is granted by stakeholders.

If I say it, they can doubt me; if they say it, it's true.

Tom Hopkins

A cause's effect on people makes it worth attention.

To a newspaper man, a human being is an item with skin wrapped around it.

Fred Allen

If the organization does not convincingly prioritize its needs, donors will.

Had I been present at the creation, I would have given some useful hints for the better ordering of the universe.

Alfonso the Wise

Appeals to pay off debt never stir the prospect's heart like campaigns to fund new initiatives.

Debt is the worst poverty.

Thomas Fuller

Acceptance of the needs removes the final barrier to philanthropic support.

Charity sees the need, not the cause.

German Proverb

The constituent must *feel the need* and be given heart by the proposed alternative.

Reality is O.K., but it's just not enough.

Charlie Quackenbush

Prospects must feel the urgency of organizational needs.

Necessity is not an established fact, but an interpretation.

Friedrich Wilhelm Nietzsche

The need for contributed support will be questioned unless the organization has looked at all alternatives.

Trust in God, but tie your camel.

Persian Proverb

Public relations and fund-raising staffs will be mutually supportive only if the organizational culture and structure provide for it.

Idealism is what precedes experience; cynicism is what follows.

David T. Wolff

Jim Norvell

Communication's effectiveness is measured by constituent response.

Self-expression must pass into communication for its fulfillment.

Pearl S. Buck

Communication consists of content, delivery, reception and interpretation.

Good communication is as stimulating as black coffee, and just as hard to sleep after.

Anne Morrow Lindbergh

Nonprofit public relations professionals must work internally as well as externally to solidify a favorable image.

Mirrors should reflect a little before throwing back images.

Jean Cocteau

If the organization does not "walk the talk,"
public relations is a thinly veiled sham.

I was not lying. I said some things that later seemed to be untrue.

Richard M. Nixon

Public relations creates the ambiance that allows linkages to develop.

It is well, when judging a friend, to remember that he is judging you with the same godlike and superior impartiality.

Arnold Bennett

Publicity is designed to get a distinct message to an identified audience within a specific time frame.

Nothing succeeds like reputation.

John Huston

Publicity is nonprofits' most under-utilized outlet for exposure.

Journalism is the ability to meet the challenge of filling space.

Rebecca West

Publicity cannot be dictated, but skilled public relations management influences it.

Ninety-eight percent of the adults in this country are decent, hard-working Americans. It's the other lousy two-percent that get all the publicity. But then we elected them.

Lily Tomlin

Promotion is the creation of attention-getting activities to gain publicity.

Don't be humble, you're not that great.

Golda Meir

Promotional tactics should be appropriate to the market sought and consistent with mission and image.

Few men have virtue to withstand the highest bidder.

George Washington

**Public relations messages should be expressed
in terms that reflect constituent values.**

It is the writer's privilege to help man endure by lifting his heart.

William Faulkner

Situational ethics aren't ethical.

I think its better to come in second than to be impeached.

George McGovern

Character is the expression ethical standards.

In matters of style, swim with the current;
in matters of principle, stand like a rock.

Thomas Jefferson

Commitment to ethical standards defines organizations and people.

If ever I said,
in grief or pride,
I tired of honest things,
I lied.

Edna St.Vincent Millay

The model of influential leaders shapes the organizational.

The manager administers, the leader innovates. The manager maintains, the leader develops. The manager relies on systems, the leader relies on people. The manager does things right, the leader does the right things.

Forbes Magazine

Nonprofits must abide by ethical standards in a much more public way than private sector organizations.

Many people like to believe charities as dishonest as they are supposedly misman-aged. They actually prefer them that way, because it means that they do not have to feel guilty about their own lack of generosity.

Benedict Nightingale

Fund raising's fiduciary implications, demand specific ethical standards of the highest magnitude.

The knights had to vow poverty, chastity, and obedience. They only kept the last vow.

Gen. George S. Patton, Jr.

Ethics are a contract between the organization and its constituents.

I only know that what is moral is what you feel good after and what is immoral is what you feel bad after.

Ernest Hemingway

Ethical conduct is influenced, but not guaranteed by standards.

My best friend is the one who brings out the best in me.

Henry Ford

The highest ideals demand the highest standards of conduct.

The ultimate test for us of what truth means is the conduct it dictates or inspires.

William James

About the Author

James R. (Jim) Norvell

Jim is a second-generation fundraiser who began his career immediately after graduating from Southern Illinois University—Edwardsville. He served in annual fund positions at Monticello College, the Foundation for Independent Colleges of Pennsylvania and Washington University before joining G. A. Brakeley & Co., Inc., Los Angeles, as a capital fundraiser. He left Brakeley to form his own capital campaign consulting firm, Development Management Associates, Inc. (DMA) and to earn his MBA at UCLA. Over fifteen years, he and partner Bob Zuer expanded DMA to $2 million in annual billings, serving clients throughout the Western United States, Great Britain and Australia.

0-595-20881-9